GRE

MYTHOLOGY

Tales of Greek Myth, Gods, Goddesses, Mythical Beasts & the Beliefs of Ancient Greece.

Adrian Myron

CONTENTS

INTRODUCTION

Greek mythology has played an important role in the history of humanity since it became part of the written record several hundreds of years ago. Many consider that the major reason for this is that the events and characters portrayed in Greek mythology give us hints and glimpses into our own human past. These stories communicate to us what our ancestors considered significant, reactions to events, and what they considered to be just or unjust. Greek mythology reflects the lifestyle and mentality of days long gone, by civilizations that were beginning to touch on the importance and consequence of human beliefs, relationships, choices, and how these opinions were reflected in our ancestors' imagination. It provides us with an invaluable understanding into the human condition of the past, just as we chronicle our activities today to provide historians of the future a glimpse in how we lived our lives.

Another reason for humankind's fixation with Greek mythology is that it includes such a wide range of diverse events populated by vibrant characters who represent a wide range of human existence. Whatever the nature of this existence, a reference will be found in Greek mythology: birth, life, conflict, tragedy, morality, relationships, family, immortality, loyalty, treachery, respect, and, of course, death. Despite being conceptualized and written such a long time ago, the drama and lessons that Greek mythology portrays reflect what it means to be human, and in some cases — especially in the case of the gods — superhuman. Every human character trait and foible can be identified within a Greek mythology character: pride, fear, confidence, loyalty, evil, good, hate, and love.

Among (the very few) critics of Greek mythology, the characters and stories that are conveyed may seem to be simply a bunch of outdated stories and over-the-top characters with no bearing on reality. Given that these chronicles were written hundreds of years ago, dismissing them as a relic of the times can be achieved with ease, and be considered not relevant to today's world. It is worthwhile to remember, however, that these tales were written not just because the authors had nothing better to do — they were sending a message about how mankind think, their behaviors, and the consequences of their actions. Therefore, these stories are still relevant today and will continue to be relevant far into the future, when coming editions of our species ruminate about Greek mythology's significance.

These fictional stories of both gods and mortals continue to captivate human beings because they were written by men who were the intellectual giants of their day. They were men who were renowned for their incisive views about philosophy, government, and human psychology. This speaks to the quality and even depth of the characters and the plot of many of the stories. Even the simple fables have a depth that can be plumbed by a discerning reader.

But we cannot overstate the value of these myths that provide us an invaluable glimpse of who we are as human beings, because the gods that the ancient Greeks invented had as much if not more moral, character flaws, and weaknesses than the humans that they held dominion over. We proceed with excitement when we realize new versions of the tales told and retold in various forms in books, magazines, movies, and television.

Probably the most well-known chronicler of Greek tales was Plato, who authored the popular dialogues *Philebus, Phaedrus, Symposium,* and his iconic *Republic.* His writings have influenced practically every aspect of human existence encompassing morality, politics, philosophy, and logic.

Another huge influence is the great poet Sophocles, who wrote over a hundred plays in his prolific career. He originated the eponymous tragedies concerning Oedipus and Electra — names that have become bywords in psychiatric circles — and Antigone. There is also the tragedian Euripides who had 18 of his plays survive. His famous Greek mythology works include stories about Alcestis, Bacchus, and Medea. Euripides' stories stood out because they portrayed strong women and these were written with surprising realism. What also made his plays and stories so notable was that they would show such depictions including resilient women with wise slaves. He had a massive influence on the concept of European tragedy and drama.

Then there is the comedic writer Aristophanes who wrote over 40 plays and whose writing was at one point considered to be the most feared weapon in Athens during his time. So influential were his writings that Plato even pointed out that his play, "The Clouds," was responsible for the trial and execution of Plato's mentor, Socrates. These and many other great minds authored works that have made them relevant in any age.

It is a testament to this relevance that Greek mythology continues to be widely taught today, with all major colleges and universities offering many courses that describe and detail its relevance in history and present life. That it is taught as both history *and* literature reflects its impact on human thinking over hundreds — if not thousands — of years. But even outside of its literary educational value, Greek mythology's characters and tales are still fascinating from an entertainment perspective. A quick search on the Internet will find that there is a vast trove of Greek mythology-themed movies and books today. The Trojan War, Zeus, Apollo, Aphrodite, Medusa, and various Greek gods seem to be part of the parlance of any point of human history.

No other literary tradition can boast of such a legacy.

CHAPTER ONE

THE EPOCHS OF GREEK MYTHOLOGY

To many, the term "Greek Mythology" evokes images of its icons. There is Zeus, a picture of an authoritative and oversized bearded deity standing on a cloud and clutching a bunch of thunderbolts as he surveys his domain; Apollo, walking on air with wings sprouting out of his sandals; or any of the bevy of pretty damsels — Hera, Aphrodite, the Amazons. A casual observer of Greek mythology might assume that these are all what Greek mythology is about. But while the presence of these characters is certainly important, they are a few among the many hundreds of characters that populate the Greek mythology universe. The multitude of characters and events can be confusing to a first-time reader of Greek mythology — and to properly understand it, one must approach with some semblance of a system.

A useful device is to divide Greek mythology into sections that roughly coincide with the chronology of the origins of its characters. With this approach, we will break down Greek mythology into roughly three epochs that approximate the chronology of its characters' evolutions.

The Age of Gods

This period starts with the beginning of life and approximates the Genesis story in the Holy Bible. It begins with a big vast nothingness, "Chaos," and the immediately resulting aftermath. In this period, the gods fought for their place in the heavens and on earth so as to assert their supremacy over nature and creation. This was apparently the time before mortals (human beings) came into existence and a time the gods lived alone with all the drama and turmoil seemingly too violent and turbulent to involve anything constituted with mortal flesh and blood.

The deity epoch includes the creation myth (discussed fully in Chapter Two), the first generations of the gods spawned by Chaos, and the fight for supremacy in the newly created world of supernatural gods.

Do note that the term "gods" is a tricky application in Greek mythology. In the vast majority of religions and beliefs, a "god" is usually expected as an overpowering, omnipresent, and highly influential divine being, usually an inanimate spirit that is not made available to the five senses.

In Greek mythology, however, with the exception of some the powerful Olympic gods, some of these deities figured prominently in conflicts and relationships involving mortals and other gods. They had their own hang-ups and domestic problems and were often burdened with the consequences of the terrible decisions they made.

Sometimes, mortals even superseded the allure of the gods. For example, the mortal Adonis could be considered the Brad Pitt of ancient Greek mythology — he was famous just for being famous and had no special powers at all — except that he was a beautiful human specimen. Meanwhile, the god Trophonius was mostly known for building the Oracle at Delphi with his brother, and actually died just six days after. He is celebrated in annual festivals in a small town in Greece.

This system of gods is comparable to the system of saints in the Roman Catholic Church, which has canonized thousands of saints that are universally recognized as sacrosanct by the Church but are well-known only in specific locations or represent some purpose. And like the Catholic saints, there are "major deities" who hold exalted places in the pantheon of Greek mythology.

The most famous of these "super-gods" are the Twelve Olympians who held sway over all creation. These Twelve deities were central to the overall Greek worship of myths, while other cities and towns had gods that were only known in their specific locales. These small, localized cults centered their legends, worship, and related activities on minor gods, nymphs, and other mythical creatures.

The Age of Gods and Men

When gods created humans, the general tone of their relationship was one of distrust and fear by the mortals of their godly masters, and disdained by most of the gods toward their lesser subjects. It approximates the Judeo-Christian world after the fall of Adam and Eve: Humans generally lived in misery and toil, children routinely dishonored their parents, and each man sought only to serve his own self-interests. The god/man era would be marked by the motto of "might meaning right" as deceit and treachery were the general daily themes, and the strongest of the strongest prevailed. This age was summed up with a pervasive sense of despair and evil. The authors wrote that in this period, the gods had completely forsaken mortals who would no longer feel indignation or shame for committing bad acts, babies would be born with gray hair, together with other assorted indignities.

The creation of human beings was as dramatic and contentious as any battle of gods could be. After the great battle of the gods

— the Titanomachy — only gods continued to populate the universe. The ruling gods finally decided that they needed mortals to populate the universe, not because the gods were lonely or wanted mortals to perform work which they didn't want to perform. They desired human (lesser) beings to exist for their own whim and amusement. It was as if they got tired of tormenting each other and wanted a whole new species to pester, annoy and control — sometimes with deadly consequences.

While the Christian/Catholic God formed humans out of the dust of the earth that He created, in Greek mythology Zeus gave the task to create human beings to two Titans, Prometheus and Epimetheus, who were spared banishment to the dreaded netherworld of Greek mythology, Tartarus. This story is loaded with drama, intrigue, treachery, and excitement. Prometheus' story is detailed in Chapter Three.

The Golden and Iron Ages of Humans

This is the period when humans were said to have lived among the gods freely and generally, and enjoyed interacting with them. There was peace and harmony during this period, and humans lived a very long life without losing their youthful appearance. After humans died peacefully, their spirits journeyed on to the afterlife, serving as guardians to surviving humans.

In this period, we see the iconic battles of the Trojan War and other conflicts. In the Greek author Hesiod's own classification of the stages of gods and men, he described the last stage of humankind, which he called the "Iron Age." This time can be likened to the fall of man in the Holy Bible — when Adam and Even were banished from the Garden of Eden.

In Greek mythology, this was an extended period of stress and hard labor. It was an era when mankind constantly fought with and oppressed each other. It was a time when morality had generally fallen by the wayside. Man is self-centered and selfish, prone to distrust and lying. Human bodies pay a price for this in the same way that the life expectancy of humans was declining from over a hundred years in the time of Moses. This was a time when mortals aged faster as they were constantly beset by life's pressures and troubles.

During this epoch's peak, humans stopped feeling any regret or shame for any oppression or wrongdoing. There was no refuge from evil, whether one was the oppressor or the victim.

As the first human age plunged to destruction, Zeus, the gods, and the goddesses had forsaken humanity as if to prepare for a great cleansing. Zeus, as with Jesus Christ in the Christian/Catholic tradition, was poised to come back to earth and destroy this existing edition of mortals, just as he had done before. This new mortal world would be a better version of the flesh and blood creatures that the gods themselves created previously.

Even as mankind needed to be eventually destroyed, they were created like the gods and goddesses before them. As it is with most creation stories, everything had to start from somewhere.

CHAPTER TWO

THE ORIGINAL GODS AND "CREATION"

E very major religious movement has its own story of how things came to be. For example, the Christian/Catholic God conjured everything up in six days, including the first mortals Adam and Eve. Islam and Hinduism also have their own traditions of how everything was created. Greek mythology contributes its own creation story — it explains how the gods came to be and how human mortals were woven into the overall fabric of cosmic events.

The major author of the creation story in Greek mythology was Hesiod, the prolific Greek poet. His works on the origins of gods and men are sometimes compared to that of Moses, who is generally considered to have written the Christian/Catholic version of the creation in the book of Genesis in the Holy Bible. While Moses' and most other creation stories usually talk of one supreme and all-powerful being, Greek mythology is chock-full of gripping drama dispersed among several deities.

Chaos, Gaia, and Uranus — the Beginning

The "Theogony" or Theogonía in Greek, meaning "the genealogy or birth of the gods," was composed by Hesiod around 700 B.C. Without giving a time frame as to how long it took to create everything (as with the Holy Bible's six-day creation process), Hesiod lyricized that everything began with Chaos, a gaping void of nothingness. It was from this nothingness that the goddess Gaia originated from, appearing to have materialized from the formless and empty ether of space. Gaia was a prolific god that begat many other gods. She is personified as a large-breasted woman from whom many progenies came.

In the typical Greek mythology incestuous twist, Gaia produced Uranus, who also became her husband. The birthing of offspring among the first gods came from just a single gender, a process called parthenogenesis.

Eros was the next to spawn and became the goddess of love. From Chaos came the dreaded Tartarus, or the terrifying and grim abyss below the earth (the equivalent of Hell to Christians and Catholics); and Erebus, where the newly dead pass through immediately. Gaia was where much of the creation of the Greek mythology deities began — along with many great stories.

Uranus, the Titans, and the Cyclops

The tales of these terrible creatures are among the most popular in Greek folklore.

Gaia, through Uranus, gave birth to the first set of Titans, which in Greek meant "large" beings. The Titans were comprised of six males — Oceanus, Iapetus, Hyperion, Cronus, Crius, and Coeus — and six females — Tethys, Themis, Theia, Rhea, Phoebe, and Mnemosyne.

After this initial dozen, Uranus and Gaia pronounced that no more Titans were to be born. Although, they were still somehow followed by the three Hecatonchires: Briareus, Cottus, and Gyges. The Hecatonchires were ugly giants, enormous in size paired with superior strength. A hundred hands and fifty heads added to their repulse. Even their father Uranus considered these creatures, his own children, as despicable abominations of creation. They disgusted Uranus so much that he hid them in Gaia's body.

Gaia also gave birth to a horde of Cyclops named Arges, Brontes, and Steropes. These beings were single-eyed giants that were also considered to be revolting creatures to Uranus.

Uranus wasn't content to let the Hecatonchires just live eternally within his wife's body. After some thought Uranus threw the three monsters into Tartarus. This betrayal angered Gaia, she plotted to exact revenge on Uranus when the time came. Deception was very common among the first gods as they struggled and strived for control over all creation.

To carry out her vengeful plan of revenge, Gaia fashioned a huge sickle and assembled her Titan son Cronus along with his brothers, and ordered them to castrate Uranus using the sickle. Only Cronus was bold enough to agree to the plan, volunteering to perform the castration himself. Gaia handed Cronus the sickle, and set up Uranus for an ambush. The mother and son duo sprung the trap startling Uranus. With Uranus now held captive, Cronus cut off his genitals with the sickle that Gaia forged, and cast the genitals far into the sea. The blood from Uranus' castration spilled down on to the earth and gave rise to Meliae, Erinyes, and Gigantes or Giants. From the blood and semen of his severed genitals, Aphrodite rose from the sea. By castrating Uranus, Cronus ascended to the throne as the King of the Titans. Gaia amazed with joy, awarded her daughter Rhea to his brother Cronus as his sister-wife.

The Birth of Zeus

Cronus added to the godly intrigue of the previous tale. Before Uranus' untimely death he had prophesied that Cronus' offspring would stage a revolt against him, in the same way that Cronus had rebelled against his own father.

Afraid that his children would commit a heinous act against him, Cronus ate all of his offspring, he had conceived with Rhea immediately in the moment of their birth. Rhea did not take too kindly to this horrific act and committed her own deceitful play. Rhea swaddled a rock in a baby's blanket in place of Zeus during the birth. Cronus obliviously swallowing the stone instead of Zeus.

With an inclining amount of lies and deception, the spectacle would lead to first great war of the Greek Gods.

The Titanomachy or "The Clash of The Titans"

The Titanomachy was the first great battle in Greek mythology and involved the first generations of gods that were generated out of Chaos in the creation story. The battle lasted 10 long years among the gods, and waged to determine who would rule the universe. It was an epic battle between generations of gods and resulted in the banishment of many deities, and the rise of the Twelve Olympians atop Mount Olympus. The Titanomachy is also more popularly known as the Battle of the Titans or Clash of the Titans, versions of which have been depicted in major novels, movies, and other media.

Rhea set the stage for the battle many years beforehand when she secretly sent Zeus to the island of Crete, where he was raised by Amalthea, widely known to be Zeus' foster mother. Cronus had believed that he had swallowed Zeus, hence unaware of Zeus' existence. When adulthood struck, Zeus returned to Greece, disguising himself as Cronus' cupbearer to gain the trust of Metis who he would later wed. He directed Metis to brew a drink; a mixture of wine and mustard, causing

Cronus to vomit in reverse order, all of the children that he had swallowed. After freeing his siblings, Zeus led them in revolt against the Titans led by Cronus. Zeus' contingent included Poseidon, Hades, Hera, Demeter, and Hestia, who were all desperate for revenge.

Zeus also released the Cyclops and the Hecatonchires from their banishment in Tartarus, and the beasts joined him in the revolt. The Cyclops forged lightning and thunder for Zeus, while the Hecatonchires hurled huge rocks at the enemy. With exception in Prometheus and Themis, the remaining Titans helped Cronus defend his crown. This gigantic battle ensued for 10 years before Zeus' army eventually triumphed over Cronus. Victorious, Zeus imprisoned the defectors and vanquished them to Tartarus, leaving the Hecatonchires as their guards. One of the Titans who fought along side Cronus, Atlas, was forced to carry out a special punishment: He had been punished to hold up the weight of the sky for eternity. This is immortalized in a bronze sculpture by the sculptor Rodin.

After the war, the three brothers — Zeus, Hades, and Poseidon — divided the universe between themselves. Hades, the oldest son of Cronus and Rhea, was awarded the Underworld. He is often portrayed with his three-headed guard dog Cerberus. Poseidon was gifted dominion over the ocean and all the waters; and Zeus, the protectorate of the air and the sky. The remaining victorious gods were gifted specific powers according to their nature. The gods left on earth were allowed to carry on as they pleased, except when Hades, Poseidon, or Zeus called them.

Some narratives indicate that Zeus gave the Titans their freedom after he secured and consolidated his power. This gave rise to the Twelve Olympians who established their residence at the top of Mount Olympus, where they would hold dominion over the universe.

CHAPTER THREE

THE GODS AT WORK AND PLAY

<u>The Twelve Olympians</u>

With Zeus regarded as the greatest and most powerful of the gods, and Poseidon and Hades ruling over the sea and Underworld respectively, the rest of the Olympians would have control over various aspects of the universe:

Hera, Zeus' wife, would be the goddess of marriage, women, childbirth, and family.

Demeter, the goddess of agriculture, harvest, fertility, and sacred law.

Athena, the goddess of wisdom, handicraft, and warfare.

Apollo, the god of music, poetry, art, oracles, archery, plague, medicine, sun, light, and knowledge.

Artemis, the goddess of the hunt, forests and hills, the moon, and archers.

Ares, the god of war.

Aphrodite, the goddess of love and beauty.

Hephaestus, the god of fire, metalworking, stone masonry, forges, the art of sculpture, and blacksmiths.

Hermes, the messenger of the gods, and also god of trade, thieves, and travelers.

Hestia, the goddess of the hearth, home, domesticity, family, and the state.

Dionysus, the god of harvest, the vine, winemaking, wine, ritual madness, religious ecstasy, and theater.

<u>Zeus</u>

No other god in Greek mythology affected the human condition than this god of gods. Although already married to his sister Hera the goddess of childbirth and marriage, he continued consorting with other deities and mortals as well. Zeus coupled with dozens of fellow deities but it was his relations with mortals that have drawn the most interest among Greek mythology enthusiasts. Many gripping tales would come from the adventures (and sometimes misadventures) of Zeus.

Greek mythology's authors made it pretty evident that the favorite pastime of Zeus and many of the Twelve Olympians male members was bedding women, both mortal and immortal. Their other mortal conquests included dozens of other humans, some of which were actually relatives of kings and queens who welcomed the prospect of their daughters bearing the progeny of the king of all kings, Zeus. To get an indication of Zeus' proclivity to bed women, the following is an alphabetical list of the women whom he had consorted with, mostly to the disapproval of Hera:

Alcmene, Callisto, Danae, Demeter, Dione, Europa, Ganymede, Io, Leto, Metis, Mnemosyne, Nemesis, Persephone, Semele, Thaleia, and Themis.

Callisto, Arcas and The Arranged Stars of The Universe

One of Zeus' more infamous trysts was with Callisto, a mortal princess from southern Greece, who seduced him by pretending to be another goddess. Her claim to fame, aside from being another Zeus concubine, was that she was transformed into a bear by an angry Hera (Zeus' wife), in which form she gave birth to a son named Arcas.

The story has a somewhat happy ending, albeit a little twisted. Arcas had become a great hunter and as he went into the woods one day, he came across his mother who was now a bear. Seeing her son after so long, Callisto rushed to greet him. Thinking that the bear would kill him, Arcas shot an arrow into Callisto's heart and killed her. Zeus, however, took pity on the two and raised them to the heavens as arranged stars, and are now known as Ursa Major and Ursa Minor, or the big and small bears.

Heracles and the Origin of the Milky Way

Hera, the aggrieved spouse of Zeus, was known to often conspire against Zeus's offspring to avenge her husband's infidelity. In one of the most famous episodes, Zeus bedded Alcmene, a granddaughter of the god Perseus who was already married to the mortal, Amphitryon. On the night that Alcmene was to give birth, Hera, aware of Zeus's adultery, convinced Zeus to make an oath that the child born that night would become High King. Hera then rushed to the pregnant woman's dwelling to slow down the birth of the baby.

Alcmene forced Ilithyia, the goddess of childbirth, to slow down the birth by making Ilithyia to sit cross-legged with her clothes tied in knots. This caused the baby to be trapped in the womb, incapable of getting out. But unknown to Hera, Alcmene was giving birth to twins, Heracles and Iphicles. Hera could have permanently delayed the birth of the twins had she not been deceived by Alcmene's servant, Galanthis. Galanthis told Ilithyia that Alcmene had already delivered the baby which surprised Ilithyia, who leapt up in surprise, undoing the knots in the process. This allowed Alcmene to give birth to both Heracles and Iphicles.

Eventually Hera, oblivious that Heracles was Alcmene's and Zeus' son, nursed him out of pity. However, Heracles suckled on Hera so strongly that Hera found it too painful and pushed Heracles away. The milk spilled and sprayed across the universe and the droplets formed the Milky Way. Heracles was gifted divine powers as he was fed the supernatural milk from Hera. Heracles would figure prominently in many important events in the anthology of Greek gods and legends.

In Roman mythology, Heracles is depicted as Hercules, synonymous to this day to male masculinity and strength. Aside from Heracles, there were other stalwart figures raised to help and protect mankind.

The Saga of Perseus

The king of Argos, Acrisius, was foretold that he would be killed by his grandson one day, and that this grandson would be borne by Danae, his daughter. Terrified that this prediction would come to pass, King Acrisius imprisoned Danae in a chamber underneath the earth. This way, she would never be able to meet a male and have intercourse, thus never having to give birth to the potential assassin of King Acrisius.

In the typical manner of the way that the gods and goddesses loved to interfere with others' lives, Zeus visited Danae as he pierced through the walls of her chamber, coming in the form of golden rain. He managed to enter Danae's body and impregnate her, and out of this "coupling" came Perseus. When King Acrisius heard about Perseus, he cast both Danae and Perseus off to the open sea on an ark to make sure that Perseus and Danae would never come near him again. But fate smiled upon Danae again as they safely landed on the island of Serifos, which was ruled by a king, Polydectes. Both mother and son were saved by Polydectes' brother, and Danae and Perseus were able to lead normal lives as Perseus grew up.

But as Perseus grew up to be a strong and attractive young man, Polydectes began to fall for his mother, Danae. Polydectes plotted to send Perseus away so he wouldn't interfere with his relationship with Danae. Polydectes, under the guise of sending Pereus on a heroic mission, had him sent far away for a dangerous if not impossible mission: Bring back the head of the Gorgon, Medusa. Polydectes was sure that Perseus would fail in this mission and perish.

Perseus and Medusa

The King of the Seas, Poseidon, had taken a big liking to a woman named Medusa who, like her two sisters, was extremely beautiful. Medusa, however, did not return Poseidon's attention and a vengeful Poseidon turned Medusa and her sisters into monsters. They were known thereafter as the Gorgons — which meant "dreadful." The Gorgons Stheno and Euryale were immortal and their sister, Medusa, the most beautiful of them all, was mortal.

The Gorgons were unleashed on earth to spread fear and terror. They took the form of females with human wings, with beautiful faces and bodies, but instead of hair, there were live venomous snakes squirming on their head. The unfortunate ones who looked point-blank at their faces were immediately transformed into stone.

Perseus knew that he had his work cut out for him. So he turned to two Olympians, Hermes and Athena, for assistance. With the help of nymphs, the two Olympians furnished Perseus with winged sandals so that he could fly to the Gorgons' lair at the end of the world. Perseus was also given a cap that gave him invisibility, as well as a mirrored shield and a sword. The mirrored shield was necessary so that Perseus could see Medusa's face without directly looking at her and thus avoid turning himself into stone.

With the help of the tools provided by Athena and Hermes, Perseus confronted Medusa and killed her. After he cut off Medusa's head, her blood spilled from her body led to the creation of two offspring: Chrysaor, represented by a huge, winged boar; and the famous winged horse, Pegasus. Perseus continued to use Medusa's head as a weapon against his enemies before finally relinquishing the head to Athena to place on her shield. Perseus returned from his quest and killed King Acrisius in fulfillment of the prophecy.

The story of Perseus and Medusa has become an inspiration for countless painters and sculptors to this day. The iconic Italian painter Caravaggio painted perhaps the most famous depiction of Medusa in the late 1500s, this artwork is displayed in Florence in the Uffizi museum. A sculpture of Perseus holding up Medusa's head stands proudly nearby in Florence's main plaza.

Perseus Saves Andromeda

Perseus also has another exciting tale attributed to him outside of his iconic clash with the Gorgons.

On the way home from killing Medusa, Perseus encountered the beautiful Andromeda who was chained to some rocks. Andromeda told him that her mother Cassiopeia had angered Poseidon by telling him that she was more beautiful than the Nereids who were part of Poseidon's royal court. The 50 Nereids were sea nymphs, spirits who traversed the ocean and were the daughters of Doris and Nereus, immortals who also lived in the oceans. They also often accompanied Poseidon, the god of the sea, and could be friendly and helpful to the sailors that they favored. But they could also be destructive as they showed with Andromeda and Cassiopeia. Because Cassiopeia had slighted his beloved Nereids, Poseidon punished her by flooding her country and sending a sea serpent to harass her people.

An oracle had advised Kind Cephus, Andromeda's father, that if he sacrificed her to a serpent, Poseidon would be appeased and would relent on the curse. Andromeda begged Perseus to save her. Perseus agreed, but only on the condition that King Cephus gave him Andromeda's hand in marriage, to which the king agreed. When the serpent came to kill Andromeda, Perseus pounced on and slew the serpent after a furious battle. Perseus was able to free Andromeda and was prepared to marry Andromeda.

Perseus then learned that King Cephus had deceived him because he had already promised to marry off Andromeda to Phineus. Phineus arrived with a small army to disrupt Perseus' and Andromeda's wedding. Perseus had been carrying Medusa's head in a bag, and pulled it out facing towards Phineus and his army, immediately turning all of them into stone.

When he arrived home, Perseus found out that his mother was holed up in a religious site hiding from King Polydectes, who still desired her. He warned King Polydectes that he still had Medusa's head in a bag and that he could use it against him. King Polydectes doubted him so Perseus pulled out Medusa's head out of the bag and turned it towards the king and all his guests, transforming them into stone.

CHAPTER FOUR

GODS AND MORTALS — STOLEN FIRE

N ot all the major characters in Greek mythology had special and extraordinary super powers. Similarly, not all of them were immortal or held court in the heavens or somewhere supernatural. The most compelling narratives in Greek mythology talk about the divine intervention by immortal deities in mortal affairs.

In Chapter Two, we already had a glimpse of how the greatest of the Olympians, Zeus, already married to his sister Hera, the goddess of childbirth and marriage, continued consorting with other deities and mortals. In this chapter, we will look at the more notable stories involving mortals in their struggles and associations with the deities that controlled their lives.

Greek mythology suggests that the gods became weary of cohabitating among, and bedding with, other deities. They eventually created humans and began a period when gods and men began to mingle freely with each other. The most common types of involvement consisted of gods seducing and even raping mortal women, sometimes resulting in heroic offspring. In this chapter, we take a look at the more prominent interactions between mortals and gods.

Prometheus

Zeus gave the task to create human beings to two Titans, Prometheus and Epimetheus, who were spared banishment to Tartarus (the dreaded netherworld of Greek mythology).

Prometheus molded the human beings out of clay, and teamed up with Athena, the goddess of wisdom and craft, who breathed life into his clay figures. Prometheus gave his brother, Epimetheus the task of providing human beings with different skills and qualities, such as speed, intelligence, agility, strength, fur, and wings. As the brothers began to distribute these gifts to all of earth's inhabitants, Epimetheus also began giving various gifts to non-humans.

Unfortunately, when it was time to give gifts to humans, the brothers discovered that Epimetheus had already handed out all the good qualities to other non-humans (living animals), leaving nothing for mankind. Prometheus, who loved humans more than the gods (as seen in his banishment of his family to Tartarus), then took it upon himself to at least give the short-changed humans the ability to stand up upright just as the gods could. He also decided to give them the ability to generate fire.

Prometheus' actions angered Zeus, who considered Prometheus' giving fire to the humans as an act of theft and treachery. Zeus meted out his punishment by banishing Prometheus to the far reaches of the eastern world. He was brought to a mountain where he would be restrained to a rock. Zeus also sent an eagle to eat Prometheus' liver, causing him great pain. Prometheus would relive this pain over and over again as his liver would regenerate over night and the eagle would return daily to inflict perpetual torment on him.

After many years of living and reliving this torment, Prometheus ran into some wonderful luck. Heracles one day happened to pass by the bound Prometheus and noticed that man's fire donor was going through some hellish anguish. Heracles quickly decided to put a stop to it. Using an arrow,

Heracles killed the eagle on its next attempt to eat Prometheus' liver.

Zeus, however, was not yet done with his anger at mortals for being granted fire by Prometheus. He decided to inflict pain and anguish to humans by using a woman, in the same vein that Eve pushed humanity into mortal suffering by enticing Adam with the forbidden fruit. This woman was Pandora.

Pandora

Zeus directed one of the Olympians, Hephaestus, to create a beautiful stunning human, Pandora, who was the first mortal woman (as with Eve in the Holy Bible). Pandora was initially bestowed with supernatural gifts from many of the Olympian gods. She was showered with fine silvery robes and awarded scintillating grace by Aphrodite and Athena, who also taught her all the fine crafts. Crowned with a magnificent headband made of gold that was crafted by Hephaestus, as well as being gifted with spring flower garlands.

Subsequently, Zeus ordered Hermes, the messenger of the gods, to curse Pandora with a lying tongue and a deceptive heart, awarding her with "a thievish character and a dog's mind." To cap off his disdain for humans as retribution for Prometheus having "given" the gift of fire from Prometheus, Zeus provided Pandora with a box (in some stories, a jar) that, unknown to her admirer Epimetheus, contained disease, suffering, toil, war, cruelty, evil, and death. This box, arrived with an alarming warning, under any circumstance this box should never be opened. But Zeus expected that man's weakness and unhealthy morbid curiosity would ultimately prevail, and so Pandora opened the box and cursed man by releasing to the world all the evil things contained in it. This action definitively and permanently separated Zeus and the gods from mortal humans.

Invention of Cultural Artifacts

Part of the great appeal of Greek mythology is how gods supposedly appropriated and even invented natural phenomena, tools, and implements for their use or for the use of mortals. These constitute the "origin" stories for many objects and ascribe the beginnings to many natural and manufactured things to the gods. Below are the tales of Tantalus and Lycaon and what they did for their piece of Greek mythological infamy.

Tantalus

Tantalus was a denizen of Tartarus, the Underworld. By many accounts, he seemed to get along with the gods until he fell from their favor by committing serious infractions that riled the gods. In one instance, he stole ambrosia and nectar from the gods to give to mortals. One of the major infractions committed by Tantalus occurred when he invited all the gods from Olympus to a banquet. For some reason, he performed one of the most repulsive actions in Greek mythology. During the banquet, Tantalus decided to kill Pelops, his son, and cooked him to be served to the gods in pieces during the feast. Zeus and the other gods were very displeased with Tantalus and decided to punish him, but not before reviving Pelops back to life. Before consigning him to Tartarus, Zeus destroyed all of his possessions by crushing them on top of a mountain. Zeus then meted out eternal punishment for the chastened Tantalus.

Zeus had Tantalus placed into a lake in Tartarus, and had him tied down. A fruit tree was on this lake just above Tantalus' reach. Because he couldn't bend to drink the water or reach high

GREEK MYTHOLOGY| **28**

enough to partake of the fruit, he was doomed to eternal thirst and hunger. When he attempted to sip a little water or eat a piece of the fruit above him, both the water and the fruit tree would move away, just far enough so he could not reach them.

From this tale came the word "tantalize," which means teasing someone with the sight of something that is unobtainable.

Lycaon and the Werewolves

Lycaon was a king of Arcadia, son of Pelasgus and Meliboea, two ancient immortals. Lycaon's troubles began when he sort of scoffed at the nature of Zeus' divinity. He decided to test the limits of Zeus' "godliness" during a visit by Zeus to Arcadia. Hell-bent on finding out if Zeus was indeed a god or simply a mortal, Lycaon served a dead prisoner's flesh to Zeus, partly roasted and cooked. To compound this insult, Lycaon even tried to kill Zeus during his sleep. Zeus did not take this lightly and turned Lycaon into a wolf.

Lycaon became the inspiration for werewolf horror stories, with a werewolf being classified as a "lycantrophe" after Lycaon.

Eurydice and Orpheus

Orpheus was the offspring of a Thracian prince and one of the Muses. Being Thracian meant that Orpheus was closely related to Ares, the god of war. But Orpheus was not warrior — he was a great musician. He was so good that his only competition came from the gods. His music was so powerful and inspirational that both animate and inanimate things went after him. Because of his skill, he enthralled the daughter of Apollo, Eurydice who also happened to be a nymph. They fell in love and got married — and later disaster struck.

As she was out for a walk one morning, Eurydice stepped on a viper that bit her, resulting in her immediate death. She was transported to Tartarus where Orpheus followed in an attempt to retrieve his one and only love. Facing many obstacles, he used his lyre and enticing music to get past Cerebrus, Hades' hound that guarded the Underworld. He eventually reached Hades and begged for Eurydice's return. Orpheus played his lyre for Hades who was touched by the music and agreed to return Eurydice, but with a single condition: If during their trip back from the Underworld, Orpheus takes just a single glance back, Hades would take back Eurydice forever. Orpheus went ahead of Eurydice and finally reached the Upper World, thinking that Eurydice was just behind him. It turned out that part of Eurydice was still deep in the caverns, and when he turned around to look at her, he had glanced back at the Underworld and violated Hades' condition.

Because he looked back, Eurydice slipped from his fingers, disappearing into the Underworld forever.

<u>Demeter and Persephone</u>

Persephone was the daughter of Demeter, the goddess of nature. One morning, Persephone was collecting flowers when all of a sudden, she was stolen by Hades and taken into the Underworld. Hades, who was ironically Demeter's brother, was so much in love with Persephone that he made one his very rare trips from the Underworld just to grab her. Demeter was terribly sad and devastated when she could not find her daughter. It is said that she looked for her daughter everywhere. She even disguised herself as an old woman, and roamed the earth with a torch in hand for nine days and nine nights, looking for her daughter.

Demeter finally met Hekate, the deity of the crossroads, spirits, witchcraft, and magic, at the dawn of the 10th day. Hekate saw the pitiful state of the desperate Demeter and told the desperate mother to seek help from the all-seeing sun god, Helios. Helios related to a disbelieving Demeter about how her brother Hades had dragged her daughter down into the Underworld. Demeter was so saddened by the news that the plants and crops ceased to grow. This caused a lot of trouble among humans who would starve if the earth stopped yielding food.

Demeter begged Hades to allow Persephone to come back up among the living, pointing out that the beautiful and young Persephone was not made out to live in the Underworld. Hades immediately questioned Zeus as to what they should do, and they agreed to let Persephone continue to live in the Underworld while coming back to earth from time to time. To determine the time for her stay between both worlds, Hades gave Persephone a pomegranate. When someone ate a pomegranate in Hades, the person who was eating the fruit would stay with Hades depending on how many seeds they swallowed. Thankfully for Demeter, Persephone only swallowed enough seeds to make her live in the Underworld for four months each year, while the rest of the time she could live with Demeter on earth. Despite the compromise, Demeter's sadness caused the earth to be infertile during Persephone's absence, and would only grow back when it was Persephone's turn to stay on earth with Demeter.

The story of Persephone and Hades is connected to the coming of spring and winter: It is springtime whenever Persephone comes to the earth and winter when she descends to stay with Hades in the Underworld.

Many festivals in Greece celebrate the saga of Persephone especially on her return from her time with Hades, including the so-called Elefsinian rites, a closely guarded secret event of which very little is known until today.

CHAPTER FIVE

THE GREAT CONFLICTS, PART I — THE TROJAN WAR

T here is no other story in human civilization, with the exception of the stories in the Old Testament and the story of Jesus Christ in the Judeo-Christian tradition, that has inspired artists of every kind and predisposition like the Trojan War. Greek educators make reading and understanding the narratives of the Trojan War compulsory classroom and study material.

The Trojan War is a definitive and iconic account of Greek mythology because it combines all the elements that have immortalized Greek mythology as the gold standard of storytelling, drama, and suspense. The Trojan War's characters include gods, demi-gods, monsters, human heroes, and villains embroiled in a long-running saga of conspiracy, deceit, murder, widespread destruction, appalling and heartbreaking deaths, and of course, inspiring redemption and victory.

The totality of the tale of the 10-year Trojan War, however, did not come from just one writer or account (even if Homer is the most significant source for the narration because of *The Iliad*), but from various corroborative textual and archaeological sources.

One single authoritative work does not cover all the details of the full story of the Trojan War. Some depictions and narratives are even contradictory, but the outline remains the same. The most important sources are *The Iliad* and *The Odyssey*, traditionally attributed to Homer, and was written sometime between the 6th and 9th centuries B.C.E. This diversity of authorship adds to the scale and scope of the apparently fictional war.

The story began in about 1200 B.C.E. when a jilted Menelaus, King of Sparta (in Greece) and the brother of Agamemnon, the King of Mycenae, organized an expedition to retrieve his wife, Queen Helen. Helen had run off with Paris, a prince of Troy, along with a massive amount of Spartan treasure. Agamemnon was at that time the most powerful leader in Greece. Helen was the daughter of Leda (from her union with Zeus) and Tyndareus, and was considered the most beautiful woman of her day. Her father, together with all the Greek warriors, promised to avenge any insult to her.

The gods were intimately involved in the Trojan War. Among the most powerful gods involved where Ares, the god of war, and Athena, the goddess of wisdom and war, who found themselves on opposite sides of the war. Athena initially favored non-violent means to settle disputes but indicated that she would go to war when absolutely needed. Ares was involved in the battles and faced off with Diomedes, the king of Argos. And while Diomedes fought Ares, Athena came to Diomedes' aid by providing him with the helm of invisibility that was borrowed from Hades. The helm caused Ares' spear to veer off-course when it was hurled towards Diomedes. This gave Diomedes the opportunity to launch a counterattack against Ares, who was seriously wounded. Ares was forced to leave the battlefield and return to Mount Olympus where he was tended to by Zeus.

The Greek Generals Attack Troy

When the Trojans refused to turn over Helen, the Greeks put together a massive army to invade Troy, where they would assemble, and leave from Aulis. Agamemnon gathered a team of Greek heroes that included Ajax, Nestor, Odysseus (in Roman myth, Ulysses), the famed warrior Achilles, and Diomedes, the king of Anatolia. With a fleet of over a thousand Spartan ships, they crossed the Aegean Sea and attacked Troy, continuing to demand the return of Helen by the Trojan king, Priam.

But Achilles, because of some disagreements with the Greeks, left the battle temporarily. This worried the Greek generals, because Achilles was part of the prophecy that Troy could not be conquered without his participation in an invasion. Achilles was an extremely fearsome and skilled warrior who went on to kill many Trojans. Some narratives have him as the lover of Helen of Troy and Medea, who would be featured in another classic Greek story of Jason and the Argonauts (which will be described in Chapter Six).

The invading Greek contingent was led by Agamemnon who had had previously insulted the goddess Artemis by an impious boast. Artemis sent strong contrary winds to hinder the invading fleet, and Agamemnon had to offer his daughter Iphigeneia as sacrifice to appease Artemis who then ceased the contrary winds and allowed the Greek fleet to sail on.

The first Greek warrior who landed on the shore, Protesilaus, was killed by the great Trojan warrior and general Hector. After they landed, the Greeks attempted another shot at diplomacy and sent a contingent to retrieve Helen and some treasure. When the Trojans refused again, the Greeks entrenched themselves for a siege that would last almost 10 years. It is in the 10th year when Homer's narrative *The Iliad* commences, and where many of the fanciful and gripping stories ensue. There are many dramas within dramas in the Trojan War, with many involving feuds between gods and mortals. Among the more prominent ones include:

Paris the Troublemaker

Paris is a major player in Greek mythology, and he pretty much comes across a detestable man, as he is generally known to have ignited the fuse that started the Trojan War. He was the son of Troy's Queen Hecuba and King Priam. His mother saw Paris as a flaming torch in a dream before he was born. Aesacus, the seer, told Hecuba that the unborn Paris would eventually cause the destruction of Troy. Aesacus added that Paris should be killed so that Troy could be saved. Through a series of fortunate events, Paris' life was spared, and he married a nymph, Oenone. Oenone promised Paris — even after he left her for Helen — that she would revive him if he was seriously injured in battle.

Paris was considered a coward and generally not a skillful warrior even as he fought in the Trojan War that he ignited. He also used a weapon that was not the favorite of the heroes and the brave — the bow and arrow, indicating that he shunned close-quarter combat.

Philoctetes eventually mortally wounded Paris, and a desperate Helen pleaded with Oenone to fulfill her promise to Paris by healing him of his mortal wounds. Oenone, however, refused to help Paris, as she was still hurting from Paris leaving her for Helen. Paris succumbed to his mortal wounds and a suddenly repentant Oenone, out of grief, plunged into the same funeral pyre that burned Paris' body.

The Feud Between Apollo, Achilles, and Agamemnon

The story of the feuds between the three As — Apollo, Achilles, and Agamemnon — is an iconic one because it once again involves a true god, Apollo. The other protagonists were Achilles, the "mixed breed" progeny of an immortal woman (Nereid Thetis), and his father, the mortal Peleus; and Agamemnon, a mortal king. It started with a feud between Achilles and Agamemnon in the final year of the war.

Following one of Agamemnon army's raids, a daughter of one of Apollo's priests, Chryseis, was captured as a prize of war by Agamemnon. Apollo's priest, Chryses, pleaded with Agamemnon to free his daughter, but his request was quickly spurned. In desperation, Chryses prayed to Apollo for the release and safe return of Chryseis. An angry Apollo, insulted by the bold move of Agamemnon, heeded Chryses' plea and unleashed a nine-day plague over Agamemnon's army. After consulting the seer Calchas and being persuaded by Achilles, Agamemnon learned that the plague could only be removed by forcing Agamemnon to sacrifice Iphigenia, his daughter. Although he reluctantly agreed, Agamemnon demanded compensation and stole Briseis, an attractive slave belonging to Achilles.

In response, Achilles, who had been fighting for the Greeks and Agamemnon's forces, threatened to withdraw from battle, jeopardizing the Greek's chances against the Trojan army. Agamemnon realized the importance of Achilles in the war effort and sent representatives to Achilles, begging him to return to action. Achilles initially refused, only be spurred back to battle when Patroclus, a close friend, was killed in battle.

Achilles and Hector

Hector, the famed general of the Trojans, was successful in many battles against the Greeks and was on the verge of pushing the enemy towards the ocean as they began to attack Greek ships, placing the Greeks on the cusp of total destruction. But the Greek warrior Patroclus led his forces against the Trojans wearing Achilles' armor and was successful in pushing back the Trojans away from the shore. Despite his apparent success, Patroclus died in battle against Hector, delaying a decisive assault on Troy.

Achilles, saddened after being told of Patroclus' death, ended his refusal to fight and asked Hephaestus, the god of blacksmiths, to fashion a new armor for him to replace the one that Patroclus was wearing before his death. Achilles carried this new instrument, the Shield of Achilles, an iconic symbol of bravery and strength to use in battle. Achilles went to the battlefield and took out many enemies, all the while hunting down Hector. He even took on Scamander, the river god, who was angry with Achilles for clogging up his water with the dead bodies of the men that Achilles had killed. Scamander attempted to kill Achilles by drowning him, but Achilles was saved by the intervention of the gods Hephaestus and Hera. Zeus then sent other gods to appeal to Achilles to prevent Achilles from sacking Troy before the appointed time, indicating that Achilles' rage could possibly change the fates destined for men.

Eventually, however, Achilles was able to locate a fleeing Hector. Hector then faced Achilles in a fight he was certain to lose, due to Achilles' superior battle skills. Hector charged towards Achilles with a sword, but failed. Before accepting his destiny in the hands of Achilles, Hector begged his adversary to respect his corpse after he is killed. Achilles refused at first and told Hector that he would hack his corpse into pieces and eat him raw to avenge the agonies that Hector had caused.

After Hector was killed by Achilles, Hector's father Priam, with the assistance of Hermes the messenger god, sought out Achilles to ask for his son's body. Achilles finally agreed and promised the end of hostilities until Hector's funeral was over.

The Final Days of Achilles

Part of Achilles' valor can be explained because of his indestructibility as a result of his mother Thetis dipping him in the river Styx when he was just an infant. Thetis held up Achilles by one of his heels and dipped his entire body in the river, rendering him indestructible except for the vulnerable heel where she held him.

In the prime of his sterling warrior career, Achilles was struck down by an arrow shot by Paris. The god Apollo is said to have directed the arrow towards the heel of Achilles, the only vulnerable part of his body. After a short quarrel as to who should receive Achilles' legendary armor, it was given to Odysseus.

The Trojan Horse

The Greeks used the "Trojan Horse," a massive hollow wooden structure that was filled with armed Greek warriors, to try to infiltrate and overrun the well-fortified Troy. To carry out this deception, the Greeks tried to make it look like they were abandoning the conflict with Troy, leaving the horse and making it appear that its forces had sailed away in defeat. The Greeks left the massive wooden horse just within the gates of the city, and the Trojans triumphantly recognized the horse as the spoils of war — a trophy of sorts. As Troy slept that night, the Greek warriors climbed down quietly from the horse and opened the gates of Troy to enable the Greek army to enter. This allowed the Greeks to overrun the shocked and surprised Trojan forces. The Greeks destroyed the city and put an end to the 10-year conflict.

In the process of sacking and destroying Troy, the Greeks murdered King Priam, together with Hector's infant son, Astyanax. Thirty of the Achaeans' best warriors had hidden in the Trojan horse's belly and two Greek spies, in its mouth.

But because Troy was given to mortals as a gift from the gods, the gods considered the sacking of Troy a sacrilege and they destroyed most of the Greek fleet as they journeyed back from Troy. In the return voyage, Agamemnon was murdered by his wife and her lover. They also killed Cassandra, Agamemnon's lover.

Helen, whose elopement with Paris started the epic war, came back home to Sparta and became queen to Menelaus once again. Some accounts tell of her banishment to the island of Rhodes after the death of Menelaus, and that she met her death by hanging upon the orders of a vengeful war widow.

The great Roman poet Virgil who, like most followers the Trojan War that were left enthralled by its scope and spectacle, authored *The Aeneid*, which tells of a group of Trojans led by the Trojan hero Aeneas. The Trojans fled their destroyed city and proceeded to Carthage to establish the city of Rome, assigning some sort of origin story to approximate the impressive myths originated by the Greeks.

CHAPTER SIX

THE GREAT CONFLICTS, PART II

While the Trojan War is widely considered as the most consequential and famous battle of gods and men in Greek mythology, there were other conflicts of smaller scale that dot the Roman mythology landscape. Many of these involve scuffles that put the so-called immortals — gods — in conflict with mortals who faced daunting odds against all sorts of obstacles, monsters, and circumstances.

Odysseus

Odysseus (Ulysses in Roman folklore) was a Greek hero in the Trojan War and was instrumental in leading the Greek forces against Troy. He is also known to be instrumental in the Trojan Horse effort that finally led to the defeat of the Trojans. But Odysseus' adventures did not end with the Trojan War. After the war, he travelled back to his home to Ithaca where he met many challenges as recounted in the Homeric poem, *The Odyssey*.

As he left for his home, Odysseus made a grievous error by revealing his identity to Poseidon's son Polyphemus, a Cyclops who caused his father to create rough seas throughout Odysseus' journey home. After Odysseus evaded Polyphemus, his ships reached the island of Aeolus, the god of winds, who put all the winds in a bag and gave the bag to Odysseus to try to safely guide his fleet. The bag did not contain the advantageous west wind, which should blow Odysseus' ships all the way to Ithaca. Here, human greed rears its ugly head.

Just before they reached their destination, the ships' crew took the bag containing the winds from Odysseus, thinking it held gold. When they opened the bag, they released all the other winds and their ship was blown away from the island — and they have returned to where they started. This time, an angry Aeolus refused to help them again, and they were left to travel on their own.

The remainder of their voyage included forays to the island of the cannibalistic tribe, the Laestrygonians, who proceeded to eat all the crew members of all the ships, even those on Odysseus' ship. Odysseus' misfortune continued as they reached the island of the witch Circe, who turned all of Odysseus' crew into pigs. Odysseus, using a magical herb given to him by Hermes, was able to resist her witchcraft, and even managed to make Circe fall in love with him. He convinced Circe to transform the pigs back into men after successfully seducing her. Staying on the island for a year, Odysseus had a child with Circe, named Telegonus. Odysseus' crew then left to continue on their voyage.

As they reached the world's western edge, Odysseus was visited by his mother's spirit, who told him to return home since his wife Penelope was being pursued by many suitors. He was given advice on how to return by the prophet Teiresias and by Circe. But Odysseus ignored the advice of Teiresias and Circes and caught the cattle of Helios, the sun god. An angry Helios told Zeus to punish Odysseus. Zeus then caused a shipwreck wherein Odysseus was the only survivor. He reached the island Ogygia where another witch, Calypso, kept him prisoner for seven years before he was released again, thanks to the god Hermes intervening on his behalf.

Upon his return to Ithaca, Odysseus found out that his wife Penelope was on the verge of choosing another husband among many suitors. Odysseus eventually convinced Penelope that he was truly her husband and killed the other suitors.

But Odysseus' life would end in tragedy. When his son with Circes, Telegonus, grew up, he travelled to Ithaca to meet his father. When he reached the shores of Ithaca, he got hungry and killed some sheep that belonged to Odysseus. Not recognizing Telegonus, Odysseus got into a savage fight with his own son and was killed.

The Revolt of the Giants

In the days before mortal men were created, a big battle ensued soon after Zeus and his brothers assumed control of the earth. The Giants, who were created from the blood spilled from Uranus' castration, attacked the Olympians to try to gain control over Olympus. There were 24 giants who participated in the attack and their size and number were of great concern to the Olympians. The Giants staged their assault by stacking up several mountains to allow them to reach the peak of Mount Olympus, where the ruling gods resided.

Heracles, who was earlier prophesied to repel a revolt against the Olympians, struck down the first Giant to reach Mount Olympus with an arrow, but the Giant was able to get back up. Athena soon figured out that the Giant survived because he was on his native ground. Athena then ordered Heracles to take the Giant to a foreign land where he could not be revived once struck down. A series of battles allowed the superior strength of the Olympians to come out victorious over the Giants.

Jason, the Argonauts, and the Golden Fleece

While not a battle in the sense of a single epic showdown like the Trojan War, the story of Jason and the Argonauts is still a gripping tale of bravery and heroism. It persists as one of the most iconic tales of Ancient Greece.

In this oft-retold story, Jason from Argo arrived in his hometown of Iolcus to find out that the throne of his father Aeson had been usurped by his uncle Pelias. So that the throne could be returned to his father, Jason agreed to retrieve the Golden Fleece from Colchis, located across the treacherous Black Sea. The Golden Fleece was made up from the hide and hair of a golden ram with wings, and was the ultimate symbol of kingship and authority.

To cross the treacherous sea, Jason decided that hehad to fashion a suitable ship for the voyage. He enlisted the help of a shipmaker, Argus, who constructed an amazing ship that could give prophecies and communicate. The ship was named Argo, and Jason's crew would be called the Argonauts.

One of the most interesting parts of the story is the makeup of the crew. It was comprised of many sons of gods and included Heracles or Hercules, the son of Zeus and one of the mightiest deities in Greek mythology. Jason's crew also included another Greek god, Pollus, who would have a significant role in battling various adversaries and threats during their voyage.

On the way to Colchis, the Argonauts faced many adventures and challenges in various islands. These included Lemnos, Doilones, and Cius, where they had to leave Heracles behind. They also travelled to Bebryces in Bosporus, ruled by Phineas; and the Sympleglades, which were really two massive stone structures that crushed ships that try to pass through them, only to encounter feisty male-hating Amazons, which they pretty much left alone for the sake of their safety.

Along the way, Jason and the Argonauts faced the gigantic and fearsome Harpies, and other obstacles strewn along their way. When his fleet reached Colchis, Jason was told by its King Aeetes that Jason could have the fleece only after he finished three seemingly impossible tasks. These included destroying dragons that came out from the bowels of the earth, and striking down the horrific dragon that stood guard over the Golden Fleece. With the assistance of Aeetes' daughter Medea and the goddess Hera, Jason succeeded, secured the Golden Fleece, and triumphantly returned home.

The Story of Oedipus

The story of Oedipus mostly comes from writings by Sophocles. While it does not consist of a titanic battle in the sense of battlefields and death, it is an often-retold story about human relations in all levels without the excessive violence that is the hallmark of most Greek mythology stories.

Oedipus was a king who ruled over Thebes, in what is now Boeotia, a city in central Greece. He was the son of Queen Jocasta and King Lauis who consulted the Oracle at Delphi to determine if he would ever have children with Queen Jocasta. King Lauis was told that any son born from their union would end up murdering them. Eventually, Queen Jocasta and King Lauis did have a son. To avoid the prophecy, King Lauis ordered his servants to pierce the baby's ankles to prevent him from crawling. They named the boy Oedipus, meaning "swollen foot."

To make doubly sure that Oedipus would not fulfil the prophecy, Queen Jocasta gave Oedipus to one of her shepherds and ordered the servant to leave the baby in the mountains to die. But the shepherd felt sorry for the baby, and instead handed him over to the court of King Polybus of Corinth and his queen, Merope. The childless royal couple decided to adopt Oedipus and raise him as their own son.

When Oedipus became an adult, he was told that King Polybus and Queen Merope were not his real parents. Disenchanted and upset, he went to the Oracle at Delphi who told him that he would eventually marry his mother after killing his father. Thinking that this meant he was prophesied to kill King Polybus and Queen Merope, who had been nothing but kind to him, he decided to go to Thebes instead of Corinth to keep his adoptive parents safe. On the way to Thebes, he encountered his biological father, King Laius, who was about to see the Oracle at Delphi. Oedipus got into an argument with King Laius' charioteer and ended up killing him and King Laius, thus fulfilling the Oracle's prophecy.

Oedipus then met a monster Sphinx, who had been plaguing Thebes by destroying crops and killing and eating any traveller who failed to answer his questions. He asked Oedipus to answer the same question that he asked other travellers: "What walks on four legs in the morning, two legs in the afternoon, and three legs in the evening?" After thinking about the question carefully, Oedipus provided the correct answer: Man. Man crawls on four legs as a baby, walks around on two legs as an adult, and uses a walking stick (a third leg) as an old man. The Sphinx, upset that his riddle was correctly answered, fell off the rock it was sitting on and died.

When Oedipus returned to Thebes, he was told by Creon, the acting king at Thebes, that anyone who would be able to kill the Sphinx would be allowed to marry the queen, Jocasta, and become king. Not knowing that Jocasta was his mother, Oedipus married her and together they bore four children: Antigone, Eteocles, Ismene, and Polynices.

Several years later, as pestilence descended on Thebes, Oedipus sent Creon to the Oracle at Delphi to consult about what to do about the pestilence. The Oracle told him that the disasters happened because Laius' killer had not been identified and caught. Oedipus then asked the prophet Tiresias to tell him who the killer was. Tiresias told Oedipus that it was Oedipus himself that killed Laius and that he did not know the identity of Oedipus' real parents. After a heated argument between Creon and Oedipus, Jocasta told them of their baby son and how he supposedly died when she ordered the shepherd to leave him in the mountains.

While they were arguing about the death of Laius, a messenger from Corinth arrived and informed everyone that King Polybus of Corinth had died. Upon hearing the news, Oedipus was relieved, thinking that Polybus was his real father and that the prophecy that he would kill Polybus did not come true. He then refused to attend the funeral to avoid meeting his adoptive mother and invalidate the second part of the prophecy.

But the messenger told Oedipus that King Polybus and Queen Merope were only his adoptive parents. Upon learning this, Oedipus was crestfallen, knowing that he had killed his biological father and married and impregnated his biological mother. He tried to see Queen Jocasta who had hanged herself. His grief knew no bounds and he took a brooch from Jocasta's gown and pricked his eyes to blind himself. He fled the city with his daughter Antigone as a guide and reached Athens, where he met and was welcomed by King Theseus. He died in Athens a short time later.

The twisted and twisting tale of Oedipus is used as a backdrop to the psychological condition called the Oedipus Complex, wherein a son has an unusual fixation or attraction towards his mother.

CHAPTER SEVEN

CREATURES, MONSTERS, AND OTHER STRANGE BEINGS

G reek mythology was not only about gods and humans, but also about many creatures and beasts that populated the earth, the heavens, and the underworld. Some were benign and even pleasant creatures, while many were malevolent and provided great danger and drama to the heroes of Greek mythology.

Cyclops

We saw in Chapter Two how the Cyclops figured in the Titanic battle among the Gods. They feature again in Odysseus' trek in his voyage back to his homeland in Ithaca. On his way back to Ithaca, storms buffeted his ships and they were forced to beach on the island controlled by the Cyclops Polyphemus. The Cyclops began to eat the crew of Odysseus's ships until Odysseus somehow managed to trick Polyphemus and blind the Cyclops, thus allowing him and his remaining crew to escape.

Nymphs

These are minor female immortal divine spirits that live in specific landforms or locations. They usually lived in lakes, streams, forests, and mountains. They were depicted as young, nubile, and beautiful women who loved to sing and dance, and are the inspiration for the fairies of other folklore.

Among the nymphs were the Nereids who formed part of Poseidon's court. These included:

Oceanids – Nymphs who populated the seas. They are the 3,000 daughters of Tetyhs and and Oceanus. Each Oceanid was a patroness of a particular cloud, flower, pasture, pond, lake, sea, river, or spring.

Meliae – Tree nymphs that were created from the semen or blood that was scattered on earth when Uranus was castrated by Cronus

Muses – The muses were nine Greek goddesses who ruled over the arts, literature, and the sciences, and offered inspiration in those subjects. They were the daughters of Zeus, the god of gods, and Mnemosyne, the goddess of memory. The nine muses were Urania, the muse of astronomy; Thalia, the muse of comedy and idyllic poetry; Terpsichore, the muse of dance and chorus; Polyhymnia, the muse of sacred poetry; Melpomene, the muse of tragedy; Euterpe, the muse of music; Erato, the muse of lyric poetry; Clio, the muse of history; and Calliope, the muse of epic poetry.

Pegasus

This winged horse sprang from Medusa's neck. Pegasus eventually flew Perseus to safety after Medusa's sisters chased him for decapitating their sister.

Minotaur

The story of the minotaur and Theseus is one of the most popular "creature" stories in Greek mythology. Theseus was the only son of the primordial kings of Athens, Aegeus. Aegeus was a man of courage and strength — qualities that seemed to have rubbed off on his son. Aegeus was also wise and intelligent, and he used his wisdom and intelligence in shrewd political maneuverings. He not only consolidated Athens under a unified political system, but his actions also helped benefit the city and the surrounding regions. Everything seemed to be humming along perfectly until one year when the spring equinox was approaching. Athens seemed to be worried and cowering in desperation. A worried Theseus had no idea what was going on, and his father refused to tell him what was wrong despite Theseus' pleas for answers.

Desperate for answers, Theseus went to the harbor and approached a black-sailed ship that caught his eye. He met the ship's captain who told him that the eldest son of the King of Crete, Minos, was killed accidentally in Athens. King Minos was looking for retribution for his son's death and demanded that a yearly tribute as compensation. Minos wanted seven young women and seven young men to be brought to the Labyrinth under the palace every year. In the Labyrinth, a dreadful and vicious monster, the Minotaur, would wait for the 14 young men and women and eat them. The Minotaur was a voracious and scary monster — half-bull and half-man, with huge horns protruding from its head.

Upon learning of this demand from King Minos, Theseus rushed to his father and volunteered to be one of the "sacrifices" to be sent to Crete. He told his father that upon reaching the Labyrinth, he would slay the Minotaur. With Theseus being the sole heir to his position and throne, Aegeus initially refused. But eventually Theseus was able to convince his father that he wanted to prove himself a hero, and that he would change the black sails of the ships to white if he returned successfully from his mission.

Upon their arrival at Crete, Theseus and his 13 other companions were welcomed by King Minos. Theseus told Minos that he was the son of the King Aegeus. Minos asked Theseus to retrieve a ring into the ocean to prove his skill. Theseus did so with the help of Thetis, a nymph.

That same night, Minos' daughter Ariadne visited Theseus and offered to help him if he promised that he would bring her to Athens with him. Ariadne explained that the reason the Labyrinth was so deadly was because people would get lost in its confusing maze until they got lost, tired out, and became easy fodder for the Minotaur. So Ariadne gave Theseus a ball of silk thread and advised him to tie one end to the Labyrinth's entrance, and unroll it as he goes around the maze, where the string would help direct him back to the entrance.

The next day, Theseus and the 13 other human sacrifices entered the Labyrinth. Following Ariadne's plan, he wrapped one end of the strong to a rock and led the others towards the center of the Labyrinth. They saw that the Minotaur was asleep. Theseus quietly approached the monster and tore off one of its horns. He then ran away after poking the beast with the horns. This wakes up and angers the Minotaur who ran after Theseus. Theseus then used the horn as a spear and hurled it at the Minotaur. The horn sliced into the beast's neck and stayed there. The Minotaur, despite being mortally wounded, still gave chase but collapsed dead eventually.

After slaying the Minotaur, Theseus returned to his father and Athens — as the hero that he said he would become.

Hellhounds

These dogs were the mascots of the god of the underworld, Hades. The lead dog Cerberus is often recognized as the "hound of Hades." Most artistic portrayals depict the animal as a three-headed dog with serpents protruding from its body, and ending with a serpent's tail. The hound acts as a sentry, guarding the gates of the Underworld and preventing any dead souls trapped there from escaping. It is said that Cerberus was the progeny of the monsters Echidna and Typhon. In Greek mythology, Heracles captured Cerberus in one of his adventures.

Triton

He is the ocean-bound version of Hermes, and is the messenger of the sea. He is the son of the gods Amphitrite and Poseidon, the goddess and god of the sea, respectively. As such, he lived in a golden palace with his parents in the depths of the sea.

He is usually shown in Greek art as having a fish's tail for his lower body, and a human's torso for the top half. Ovid the writer has depicted him as having seashells barnacled on his shoulders. He has fins all over his body, including the human top half.

His special attribute is his conch shell, twisted and large, which he blows like a trumpet to control waves, either calming them or making them turbulent. His conch can make a loud cacophony, sounding like a huge and dark beast that is said to make giants flee. Like his father, Poseidon, he carried a trident.

He figures in the adventures of Greek heroes, helping guide the Argonauts to find passage back to the sea after they were lost and wandering in the desert.

The Oracle at Delphi

The Oracle of Delphi, recognized as "Phytia," served in the Temple of Apollo as a high priestess. While not a creature or animal, the high priestess of Apollo's Temple at Delphi was a mysterious and inscrutable being who seemed to be neither a part of the gods nor part of the mortals. She served as an oracle, seer, and prophet, and was consulted by many characters in Greek mythology, including Lycurgus and Oedipus. She was the most authoritative oracle and seer among the Greeks and her name is often mentioned in Greek mythology whenever anybody wanted to get an answer to a problem, or to look for something or someone.

The Amazons

We have seen that women figured prominently in the legends of the gods and mortals in Greek mythology. This aspect is what sets it apart from other traditions like Judaism, Islam, and Christianity that consign women to the background and giving males the run of the drama. Many iconic stories in Greek mythology center around women and their adventures. The Amazons were said to originate from around the Black Sea in a land called Themiscrya in what is modern-day Turkey today.

The all-female Amazons have been generally portrayed as men-haters, being a tribe made up wholly of women, and living separately from man. However, the Amazons were not capable of spontaneous creation or parthenogenesis, as the primordial gods were. As such, in order to "reproduce" and replenish their tribe, they needed to pay annual visits to the Gargareans, a nearby tribe comprised solely of men. Both the Gargareans and the Amazons needed each other to survive so they procreated and distributed their male offspring to the Gargareans, and the female offspring to the Amazons. When any males were born, they were either slain by the Amazons, left to die in the wilderness, or returned to the Gargareans. If any male strangers or travelers happened to pass by, they could choose to stay with the Amazons only if they agreed to be the lowliest of servants, and relegated only to do the most menial of jobs.

But first and foremost, the Amazons were fierce warriors who possessed excellent battle skills. They were more than a match for males with their ability and strength. As such, they spent a great majority of their waking hours strengthening their bodies and sharpening their battle skills, making sure that they were prepared for any attack or battles.

The most notorious Amazon queens were Hippolyta and her sister, Penthesilia. Penthesilia fought against the Greeks in the Trojan War, and was supposedly gifted by Ares a magic girdle which gave the wearer special powers. In the 10th and final year of the Trojan War, Achilles slayed Penthesilea along with many other victims, and the Amazons had to retreat together with the other Trojans after the Greeks had soundly beaten them.

CHAPTER EIGHT

OTHER STORIES IN GREEK MYTHOLOGY

Aesop's Fables

While not spun in the mythic and epic proportions of the gods and heroic mortals of "traditional" Greek mythology, the stories of Aesop still resonate to this day as valuable moral tidbits that apply to humanity of any era. Aristotle, among others, indicated that Aesop was born around 600 B.C. in Thrace, which could be found along the Black Sea coast. Tradition also says that Aesop was a slave in the ancient city of Samos, and that he served masters named Iadmon and Xanthus. He eventually must have been freed and able to relate his stories, given that influential figures like Aristotle and Herodotus talked of his stories.

Aesop's tales are extremely simple stories involving mostly inanimate objects and animals that speak and are meant to convey moral lessons about life in general. Many of the stories have been used throughout the centuries as cautionary tales for questionable human behavior, including "The Boy Who Cried Wolf" and "The Tortoise and the Hare."

Icarus

The story of Icarus is also a fable that is a cautionary tale on disobedience and pride. Icarus was the son of Daedalus, the master craftsman who created the Labyrinth which held the dreaded Minotaur. Icarus tried to flee Crete using wings that his father had made from feathers waxed together. Daedalus had warned Icarus of becoming complacent and arrogant and to fly neither too high (as the sun would melt the wax) or too low (as the dampness of the sea would clog the operation of the wings). But Icarus ignored his father and flew extremely high anyway. The heat from the sun melted the wax holding the wings together and Icarus fell into the sea.

Sisyphus

Sisyphus was the founder and first ruler of Ephyra. He was a proponent of commerce and navigation but was not well-liked because he was deceitful, crafty, and avaricious. In violation of Zeus' commands, he sometimes murdered travellers and guests and delighted in the slayings because these allowed him to stay in power and ruthlessly get rid of enemies.

Eventually, however, he was punished for his evil ways. Sisyphus was given an unusual penalty. He was made to roll a massive boulder up a hill, only to have the boulder roll back down as he neared the top of the hill. He was condemned to repeat this task for all eternity. Even today, a task that seems futile and extremely laborious is described as "sisyphean." The word refers to an arduous exercise that has no hope of being accomplished.

King Midas and the Golden Touch

The story of Midas is another one that comes as a cautionary tale. Midas was a king who performed a good act on a satyr which made Dionysus, the god of wine, grant him a wish. The greedy Midas wished that whatever he touched would turn to gold. Before granting this wish, Dionysus tried to discourage him and warned him that it could spell trouble and even doom. But Midas could not be swayed. He argued that it was the best wish that he could ask for, and Dionysus had no choice but to grant it.

Upon receiving the gift of gold, Midas happily moved around touching everything and transforming then into precious gold. He realized that he might have made a big mistake when he tried to pick up some food to eat, only to realize that he could not eat it. He now feared that he was going to starve.

Midas' daughter saw the sadness of her father and, in her desire to console him, threw her arms around him, instantly herself turning into gold. It was then that he realized that the "Midas touch" was not a blessing but a curse. Disconsolate, he rushed towards the river and cried, turning the sand on the riverbanks yellow. The sadness and despair of the blessing had turned into a curse.

Phaeton and the Sun God

Helios, the sun god, had a youthful son, Helios, whom he adored. Phaeton begged Helios to allow him to drive the sun chariot. Reluctantly, Helios handed Phaeton the reigns even as he worried about his son's inexperience in driving a chariot. Helios' worst fears were realized when the inexperienced and confused Phaeton caused the immortal steeds and chariot to veer out of control. The sun chariot set the earth on fire, and the African plains were torched to desert conditions and its inhabitants, charred black.

An angry Zeus, appalled by the devastation wrought by Phaeton, struck the boy with lightning, and then hurled his burning body into the Eridanos River. His sisters assembled on the banks of the river where they were changed into amber-teared poplar trees as they were mourning the loss of their brother. They were thereafter called the Heliades.

Phaeton was placed among the stars after his death and is seen as the constellation "Auriga" meaning "The Charioteer."

Cadmus and the Founding of Thebes

Europa was the daughter of the King of Phoenicia. One day, she was carried off by Zeus and her crestfallen father sent off her brother Cadmus to look for her. After a futile search, Cadmus consulted with the Oracle at Delphi who demanded that he give up his search, and instead follow a cow, then build a city on the spot where the cow would lay down. The cow led him to Boeotia where he established the city of Thebes as foreseen by the Oracle. It is here where the city of Thebes would sprout up — the city which the famous tales of Oedipus and Dionysus would come from. Also, according to tradition, Cadmus brought the alphabet to Greece from Phoenicia.

CONCLUSION

G reek mythology has pervaded almost every aspect of our daily lives in the modern age. The heroes, events, and characters have subliminally penetrated our modern-day psyche. We take the gods, heroes, villains, and anti-heroes all in stride as if they have always been part of our lives. We are exposed to Greek mythology-oriented terminology in science and technology, enjoy commercially branded products, watch television shows and movies, read all kinds of periodicals, use our gadgets — without even realizing that we are experiencing throwbacks to the glorious fables and stories from ancient times. We watched as Apollo 11 brought the first man on the moon, ignoring that it was named after one of the Twelve Olympic gods. We forget what we were being taught the rudiments of astronomy — that most of the planets in our solar system are named after Greek gods (or their Roman counterparts).

Iconic consumer products today are even named after characters and events from Greek mythology: Amazon.com, Trident gum, Pandora Jewelry, Hermes clothing, Midas brakes, and even the National Football League's Tennessee Titans.

Greek mythology is still very much a part of our learning experience. The study of Ancient Greece is a must for students and scholars of history, philosophy, archaeology, and literature. Since it is the seat of human intellectual learning, the study of Ancient Greece is required because so much of its intellectual output continues to elicit discussion today. And because scholarly work on the arts and sciences frequently make allusions to Greek mythology, it is apparent that the appreciation of Greek mythology is essential to understanding the thought process of the ancient Greeks.

When we immerse ourselves in Greek mythology, we sometimes lose sight of the fact that everything we are reading about the gods and heroes in its pantheon is purely fiction. While there have been recent discoveries possibly suggesting that much of the Trojan War was actual historical fact, the gods and goddesses described in Greek mythology are mostly simple figments of the imagination of the ancient Greeks. They are truly myths — hence mythology — but great and wonderful mythology, and we sometimes get truly immersed in their drama.

We are outraged when Zeus treats mortals like throwaway rags and revel in the triumph of Perseus as he severs Medusa's head. We laugh at and pity the very human hubris, stupidity, and follies of major characters such as Tantalus and Icarus and are amused that they were created by the wonderful writers and poets as divine gods subject to human foibles and weaknesses. A lot can be learned from these myths, including lessons and warnings that we can apply to our daily lives. They are fiction, but this is the kind of fiction that is still useful in the modern age.

Ultimately, who can say that the fiction-based belief systems of the ancient Greeks were unfounded factually and especially spiritually? Christians, Jews, Hindus, and Muslims have their own belief systems that focus on inanimate and even supernatural deities. If we transported a time traveler from ancient Athens to today's world, he or she may look at organized religion in its current state and consider them just as unbelievable as the fantasy world populated by the likes of Zeus, Poseidon, Apollo, etc.

While we can debate the historical, moral, and spiritual values of Greek mythology, there is one non-debatable aspect — that it has made significant contributions in much of classic and modern literature in the form of symbols, and to current-day entertainment and escapism. While we may not believe that Zeus, Ares, Aphrodite, the Titans, and the rest of the characters really existed, there is nothing wrong in enjoying them in our imaginations.